DATE DUE

Street Luge Racing

by Pat Ryan

Content Consultant:
Bob Pereyra
President
Road Racers Association for International Luge

CAPSTONE PRESS
MANKATO, MINNESOTA

C A P S T O N E   P R E S S

<u>818 North Willow Street • Mankato, Minnesota 56001</u>
http://www.capstone-press.com

Printed in the United States of America.

Library of Congress Cataloging-in-Publication Data
Ryan, Pat.
    Street luge racing/by Pat Ryan.
    p. cm. -- (Extreme sports)
    Includes bibliographical references and index.
    Summary: Introduces the history and development of the sport that combines skateboarding and ice luging.
    ISBN 1-56065-538-0
    1. Street luge racing--Juvenile literature. [1. Street luge racing.]
I. Title. II. Series

GV859.82.R93 1998
796.21--dc21

                          97-11338
                            CIP
                            AC

Editorial credits
Editor, Michelle L. Norstad; Cover design, Timothy Halldin; Photo research, Michelle L. Norstad

Photo credits
Patrick Batchelder, cover, 16, 18, 21, 22, 29, 30, 34, 37, 47
John Lewis, 13, 14, 24, 40
RAIL Inc. & SLED Int., 4, 7, 8, 10, 27, 32, 38

Table of Contents

Chapter 1

Street Luge Racing

Street luge racing combines ice luge racing, skateboarding, and auto racing. Ice luge racing is a winter sport. An ice luge is a sled that slides on iron blades over ice. A street luge is a wooden or metal sled with skateboard wheels. A street luge is usually about eight feet (2.5 meters) long. With a hill, a board with wheels, and the right equipment, anyone can be a street luge racer.

Street luge racing brings speed to the streets. In street luge racing, speeds of 60 to 70 miles (97 to 113 kilometers) per hour are common. The record speed for a street luge racer is 78 miles (126 kilometers) per hour.

Street luge pilots race down hills. A pilot is someone who steers or controls something. Street

Street luge racing brings speed to the streets.

lugers also race because they love adventure. Mostly, they love to go fast.

Most street luge pilots are professionals. A professional is a person who receives money for taking part in a sport or activity. A professional also has a high level of skill.

Amateurs love street luge racing, too. An amateur is someone who takes part in a sport for pleasure. This sport raises the body's adrenaline levels. Adrenaline is a chemical the body produces when a person is excited.

Street Luge Basics

A street luge pilot puts on a helmet and safety equipment at the top of a hill. The pilot sits on the board and pushes off with the hands. Then the pilot lies on the back and steers the luge. The pilot steers the luge by leaning left or right. The harder the pilot leans to the side, the sharper the street luge will turn. The pilot stops the luge by dragging the shoes on the road.

Gravity is the force that pulls things to the earth. Gravity speeds up a street luge. But friction

A pilot steers the luge by leaning left or right.

slows it down. Friction is the force created by a moving object as it rubs against a surface. A pilot's feet also cause friction as they rub against the road. Friction helps a pilot stop a sled, even at high speeds.

Chapter 2

History of Street Luge

No one knows for sure when or where street luge racing started. Many people think it started in the 1950s in California or Washington. It may have begun when someone sat on a skateboard and rode it down a hill.

Early street luge racers started racing in a sitting position. But this slowed them down. They discovered they went faster if they laid down on the board. This is how modern street luge racing began.

In the 1970s, a man named Bob Pereyra created his own street luge sled. He traced the outline of his body on a piece of cardboard. He used the outline as a pattern to build a light metal sled. Once the sled was finished, Pereyra added

Early street luge racers started racing in a stitting position.

two sets of skateboard wheels. Then he rode the sled down a hill.

Today, Pereyra is considered one of the pioneers of street luge racing. He helped write the first rules for street luge racing. He also founded the first official street luge racers club.

Going Public

Many city governments considered street luge racing unsafe. Some city officials passed laws against racing on city streets. At this time, all street luge racers were considered outlaws. An outlaw is someone who does not obey the law. They gave street luge racing a bad name.

A turning point came in the late 1970s in Signal Hills, California. A street luge went out of control during a race. It hit and hurt some people who were watching the race. Some people call this day Bloody Sunday.

After the accident, street luge racers knew the sport would have to change. They would have to pay more attention to safety. If they did not, street luge racing might never become an accepted sport.

Today, Bob Pereyra (center) is considered one of the pioneers of street luge racing.

In 1990, Pereyra started the Road Racers Association for International Luge (RAIL). RAIL brought street luge racing to the public's attention. The association worked with cities to make the sport safer. In 1993, RAIL held the first professional street luge race.

The race occurred at the Laguna Seca Raceway in Monterey, California. It featured 22 of the world's fastest street luge racers. The race was a big success. It helped show people that street luge racers were skilled and talented athletes. An athlete is someone who is trained in a sport or game. The race showed others that athletes wanted the sport to be safe.

Street Luge Racing and Advertising

In 1994, Pereyra was watching a television commercial. The commercial featured an extreme skier jumping over a cliff. Pereyra called the company that had filmed the commercial. He told company leaders about the fast action of street luge racing. Within three days, the company

The first professional street luge race was held at the Leguna Seca Raceway in Monterey, California.

called Pereyra back. The company wanted him to do a commercial for them.

Pereyra raced down steep hillsides in Hawaii. A film crew taped him as he raced. The company used the tape in a commercial. People all over the world saw the commercial. Most saw street luge racing for the first time.

The commercial was popular. People wanted to see more of the sport. Sports programs featured street luge racing. More people became interested in the sport. Within three years, street luge racing went from a little-known sport to a recognized sporting event.

In just three years, street luge racing grew to become a recognized sporting event.

Chapter 3
Competition

Regular street luge racing can occur almost anywhere. Racers can use a parking lot or a road when there are no cars around. All they need is a smooth slope.

Extreme street luge racing requires much more. Closed mountain roads or smooth, downhill race courses are required for good racing. A race course is a route chosen for a race. Race courses provide steep slopes. On steep slopes, racers go faster.

Most street luge race courses feature many L-shaped turns. An L-shaped turn is a part of the race course that curves sharply to the left or right. These turns make the race more challenging. Racers have to control their speed when attempting an L-shaped turn. If they do not, they may wipe out. Wipe out means to fall off or crash.

Most street luge race courses feature many L-shaped turns.

In the mass luge race, a group of street lugers race downhill at the same time.

Competitions are often held on mountain roads. A competition is a contest between two or more athletes. The race course is made as safe as possible before a race. The course is closed to cars and trucks. Hay bales are placed along the course. They cushion pilots if they crash. Viewing areas are set up at safe distances from the course. For safety, people watching the races stand behind walls or fences.

Types of Races

There are many street luge racing events. The most common event is the dual luge race. Dual means two. In a dual luge race, two pilots race each other down a race course. The first to cross the finish line wins.

The LeMans challenge is patterned after a French auto race. Before the race, racers place the street luges at the starting line. The racers wait across a road from their luges. When a horn sounds, the racers run to their street luges. They climb on and push off down the hill. The first racer to the finish line wins.

In the endurance challenge, pilots race on a course that is several miles long. Endurance is how long a person can continue to do something. A car takes the racers back to the top of the course at the end of each run. A run is one ride from the start of a course to the finish. Endurance challenges can include up to five runs. Whoever has the fastest total time wins.

In the mass luge race, a group of lugers race downhill at the same time. Some mass luge races include more than 20 racers. Others have as few as four racers at once.

The X Games

The Extreme Games is a competition featuring many extreme sports. The games are shown on television. Street luge racing is one of the featured sports.

The Extreme Games are also called the X Games. They include the Summer and Winter X Games. Street luge racing is part of the Summer X Games. The athletes try to win money in the X Games.

The X Games were first shown on television in 1995. The X Games made street luge racing more popular. The sport is one of the most-watched events of the X Games.

Adults who race well can enter the X Games. Men and women can race together. The street luge races in the first X Games featured pilots from all over the world. The first races had 32 pilots. No female street luge racers competed the first year. Today, more women compete in street luge racing.

Street luge racing is one of the most-watched events of the X Games.

Chapter 4

Equipment

To win races, street luge racers must choose the best sled. To do this, they must understand physics. Physics is the science of motion, speed, and friction.

Gravity causes luges to accelerate. The luges accelerate as they move downward through a course. But wind resistance pushes against the pilots and the street luges. Wind resistance slows luges down. Wind resistance is the force of the air that pushes against moving objects. Friction slows the luges, too.

Designers use science to reduce friction. Designers are people who plan and build luges. One way designers reduce friction is to make the wheels larger. Because of their size, larger wheels create less friction than smaller wheels. The weight of the street luge also has an effect on

To win races, street luge racers must choose the best sled.

friction. A lighter sled moves faster. Street luge designers try to make the lightest possible sled.

The Luge

The luge is the most important piece of equipment used in street luge racing. Most street luges are about eight feet (2.5 meters) long and about 16 inches (41 centimeters) wide. Street luge sleds weigh 25 to 30 pounds (55 to 66 kilograms). In some places, luges are only 5/16 inch (8 millimeters) off the ground.

The Chassis

The street luge is also called the chassis. A chassis is the frame of the street luge. The chassis includes the body pan and the headrest. The pilot lies back in the body pan. The body pan is built to fit the pilot's body. The headrest supports the pilot's head. The chassis is usually made from light, high-quality aluminum. Aluminum is a light, silver-colored metal. The chassis is about one-eighth inch (3 millimeters) thick.

The chassis is the frame of the street luge.

The Wheels

Wheels are also important parts of a street luge. Most street luge wheels are made of urethane. Urethane is a type of hard rubber or plastic. The wheels are measured in millimeters. They are usually 70 millimeters (about two and three-quarters inches) across.

The wheels are attached to nylon hubs. A hub is the center of a wheel. The wheels and hub are attached to the truck. A truck is a T-shaped device that attaches the wheels to the sled.

Wheels must fit tightly on their hubs to reduce friction. Friction creates heat. At high speeds, the heat from friction is high. If there is air between the wheel and the hub, friction will heat the wheel. Some wheels have exploded from this heat.

Wheel manufacturers make harder and softer wheels. Softer wheels are the most often used. Softer wheels make the luge go faster. But sometimes wheels become even softer with use. Soft wheels heat up quickly and may make the luge hard to steer. This can cause accidents. To avoid danger, street luge racers must replace their wheels often.

At high speeds, wheels heat up quickly and may make the luge hard to steer.

Other Parts of a Street Luge

The pilot's feet rest on foot pegs. Nerf bars attach to the foot pegs and wrap around the front of the luge. They are covered with rubber. Without the nerf bars, the foot pegs would stick out. Nerf bars help keep the luges from hooking each other during a race. Hooking occurs when two street luge sleds become tangled together.

Hooking is a danger when racers draft. During drafting, one sled closely follows another. The front luge reduces wind resistance for the luge that is following. This helps the racers in the back go faster. Experienced racers use drafting to pass racers ahead of them. Passing can be dangerous. A passing racer's sled can hook the sled of another racer. Hooked racers often wipe out or cause problems for other racers.

Handlebars add to the safety of a street luge sled. In the early days of street luge racing, designers used bicycle handlebars. Today, handlebars are made especially for street luges. The handlebars are located on each side of the body pan. They point toward the pilot's feet.

Experienced street luge racers use drafting to pass racers ahead of them.

Pilots hold the handlebars to help them steer and to keep from falling off the luge.

At speeds of nearly 80 miles (129 kilometers) per hour, safety is the most important element. Designers make luge sleds with safety in mind. Street luge racers also wear special clothing for protection.

Helmet

324

Simple
Shoes

BATES
D2D
Simple

Gloves

Chassis

Chapter 5
Safety

Street luge racing is a dangerous sport if it is not done correctly. Racers and street luge clubs work together to keep the sport safe. They do this in many ways. They make rules that street luge racers must follow. These rules say racers must wear the proper gear while racing. Gear is equipment or clothing. It includes shoes, helmets, and uniforms.

Clubs and racers work together in other ways, too. Racing officials choose race courses carefully. A race course that is too dangerous will not be used. A course that is very steep is dangerous. Hay bales set up along the course protect the racers.

Gear

Street luge racers wear special gear to help keep them safe. All pilots use motorcycle helmets with

Street luge rules say racers must wear the proper gear while racing.

full face shields. The face shields attach to the fronts of the helmets. They protect the lugers' faces and eyes. Lugers can see through the shields. Helmets help protect pilots' heads, in case of accidents.

The pilots' bodies also need protection. Racers wear light, tight-fitting leather suits. These are one-piece suits that cover the racers' bodies. These suits have padding in the spine and seat for extra protection. The tight leather suits also reduce wind resistance.

Street luge racers wear leather gloves to protect their hands. These gloves have padding in the palms. The padded gloves help pilots push off harder to start down a hill. If a pilot wipes out, the gloves keep the hands from becoming skinned or cut. Knee and elbow pads also protect the pilot during a race.

Pilots wear tennis shoes to protect their feet. Some pilots wear motorcycle boots. Others wear auto racing boots, which have a pad of extra rubber on the bottom.

Street luge racers wear helmets, gloves, and leather suits for protection.

Both shoes and boots act as the street luge's brakes. Pilots stop by dragging their feet along the ground. Sometimes, pilots will glue a piece of rubber tire to the bottoms of their shoes. This helps them stop easier and makes their shoes last longer. The shoes wear out quickly. Many pilots need new shoes after every race.

Beginning With a Skateboard

Professional street luge racers seem to speed down race courses. These pilots are highly trained. They have practiced and raced for a long time. But they did not start out being so fast and talented.

Professional street luge racers began as amateurs. Many of them began by learning on skateboards. A skateboard is made to go slower than a street luge.

Pilots sit on skateboards and ride them downhill. This helps street lugers learn to control a board. It is easier to steer a skateboard than a street luge. Next, they lie back on the

Pilots stop street luges by dragging their shoes on the ground.

skateboards. This helps them get used to controlling a board while lying down. With practice, street luge racers improve their skill and speed.

Most skateboards have softer wheels than street luges. These limit speed because they create more friction. Skateboards go no faster than about 40 miles (65 kilometers) per hour. Professional street luge racers can go almost twice that speed.

Beginning to Street Luge Race

People interested in street luge racing can join clubs. There are several clubs in the United States and Canada that help people learn to street luge race.

In clubs, trainers give lessons to help new street luge racers improve. Techniques and safety are taught to keep the sport safe. Technique is a style or way of doing something. New street luge racers learn on a safe race course. They may ride only the bottom half of a

Professional street luge racers can race down hills at speeds of 60 to 70 miles per hour.

course. This limits the pilots' speed until they are ready to go faster.

Often, clubs allow people to race as amateurs. After one season, they may be allowed to race as professionals. Pilots keep practicing even after they become professionals. Street luge racers learn new techniques and improve their speeds. Their goal is to get better, go faster, and remain safe.

Pilots keep practicing even after they become professionals.

Words to Know

adrenaline (uh-DREN-uh-lin)—a chemical the body produces when a person is excited

amateur (AM-uh-chur)—someone who takes part in a sport for pleasure

athlete (ATH-leet)—someone who is trained in a sport or game

chassis (CHASS-ee)—the main part of a street luge; includes the body pan and the headrest

competition (kom-puh-TISH-uhn)—a contest between two or more athletes

draft (DRAFT)—to follow closely behind another racer

dual luge (DOO-uhl LOOZH)—a race between two luge pilots

endurance (en-DUR-enss)—how long a person can continue to do something

foot pegs (FUT PEGZ)—a place on the street luge where pilots rest their feet

friction (FRIK-shuhn)—the force created by a moving object as it rubs against a surface

hooking (HUK-ing)—when two street luges become tangled together

mass luge (MASS LOOZH)—a race where a group of sledders race downhill at the same time

outlaw (OUT-law)—a person who does not obey the law

pilot (PYE-luht)—a street luge driver

professional (pruh-FESH-uh-nuhl)—a person who receives money for taking part in a sport or activity

race course (RAYSS KORSS)—a route chosen for a race

run (RUHN)—one ride from the start of a course to the finish

technique (tek-NEEK)—a style or way of doing something

truck (TRUHK)—a part of a luge that attaches the wheels to the sled

wind resistance (WIND ri-ZISS-tuhnss)—the force of the air that pushes against moving objects

wipe out (WIPE OUT)—to fall off or crash

To Learn More

Allen, Missy and Michel Peissel. *Dangerous Sports*. New York: Chelsea House, 1993.

Brimner, Larry Dane. *Bobsledding and the Luge*. New York: Children's Press, 1997.

Tomlinson, Joe. *Extreme Sports: The Illustrated Guide to Maximum Adrenaline Thrills*. New York: Smithmark Publishers, 1996.

Useful Addresses

Road Racers Association for International Luge (RAIL)
18734 Kenya Street
Northridge, CA 91326

International Gravity Sports Association (IGSA)
638 North Crestview Drive
Glendora, CA 91741

Extreme Downhill International (EDI)
1666 Garet Avenue #308
San Diego, CA 92109

Extreme Gravity Sports
2928 Langley Crescent
Prince George, British Columbia
V2K 3J8
Canada

Internet Sites

North East Street Luge Main Page
http://members.aol.com/raptordg/luge/luge.htm

**STREETLUGE: Welcome to the home of
  Street Luge**
http://www.streetluge.com/

Extreme Gear (2)—Street Luge
http://homearts.com/pm/downtime/05xtrmb1.htm

ESPNET SportsZone: Street Luge
http://ESPN.SportsZone.com/editors/xgames/luge
  /index.html

HAE Streetluge Page
http://www.skateluge.com/stluge.htm

EXTREME
http://www.extreme-sports.com/index.html

Street luge pilots race because they love the adventure.

Index